POP ART REVOLUTION

From Novice to Artist in Simple Steps

Nicole Anthony

Table of Contents

CHAPTER ONE

INTRODUCTION

A forerunner to current craftsmanship Present day craftsmanship is maybe of the major improvement in craftsmanship of all time. The obvious advancement began during the 1950s and procured universality during the 1960s in both the US of America and England as draftsmen drew inspiration from business and standard society to make strong pieces that unequivocally reflected those pieces of everyday presence. American client culture, backing and virtuoso culture, and post bellum culture all significantly affected American pop craftsmanship. The improvement began as a moderate against elitism and regular creative standards and was a response to the business visionary and commercialization culture in post bellum America. From a wide perspective, it was an arrangement for a social change to break individuals out of their standard schedules and distance. Skilled workers headed out to Hollywood films, prominent music, comic books, and advancements for pop craftsmanship since they were really spellbinding and had more effect. Monstrous partners of the advancement consolidate Andy Warhol, Richard Hamilton, and Roy Lichtenstein, who've made shameful pop workmanship designs generally around embedded into our lifestyle. The montage "Decisively What Makes Today Homes So

Noteworthy, So Captivating?" is seen as trustworthy by numerous people might have started the progression in 1956 in London. Additionally, he depicted the characteristics of the development: "Pop workmanship" proposes: Is pop craftsmanship still important today in light of everything? Remarkable, temporary, pointless, insignificant expense, effectively made, enthusiastic, adroit, connecting with, gimmicky, alluring, monstrous systematic at no other time. From stock activities to workmanship grandstands, pop craftsmanship is all over. Experts today continue to incorporate pop craftsmanship structures into their procedures, including mark sensible effects like sprinkled, strong regions for serious for blends, spots, and striking social verbalizations using standard things. Street experts like Banksy have shown pop craftsmanship influence in their work using near stencil and visual correspondence style. Pop craftsmanship is correct right now saw as fundamentally beast in the relentless business locale. In 2013, Andy Warhol's Twofold Calamity (Silver Minor Difficulty) sold for a cerebrum blowing $104.5 million.

WHAT IS POP WORKMANSHIP

With broadcasting, serious strong regions for streams, and inventive overlays, pop craftsmanship instilled typical customary presence and things. The dynamic quality of the style looks great on everyday items like soup cans, traditional items, a pack of gum, and gadgets. Media can also imagine newspapers, magazines, and youth-oriented television shows. Pop craftsmanship made fair and standard articles into momentous ones, totally upsetting the inventive principles and social created improvement that was set up by then. Considering its zingy and energized groupings and models, outrageous symbolism from prominent media and things, and the innovative imaginative systems that depicted the pop craftsmanship style, pop craftsmanship is rapidly obvious and can be spotted from a fair ways. It frequently made use of pictures, overlays, pieces, and overt repetition, with incredible reds, blues, and yellows in the center. Furthermore, pop craftsmanship supported craziness and humor, which is the reason the vast majority of the pieces are so enrapturing. Experts used satire to slander models and tumults, shed light on late developments, and cause a couple of unsettling influences. However, there are significant differences between the development of the improvement in the United States and in Britain due to the fact that there was a significant American influence in Groundbreaking England at the time and that many of the greatest names of the improvement were American. In any case, there are different divisions.

Pop craftsmanship in the US uses common reality, normal society, vulnerability, and humor. American pop workmanship was a consequence of the chance of the Mission for charm. Roy Lichtenstein and Andy Warhol were two of the most striking and highly educated pop artists from the United States. Obviously, the improvement's early phases in Britain were discrete by a more instructive bowed. English pop workmanship was directed by American culture as of now through a substitute, more distant spot of connection. To inspect the western blueprint of control, which influenced social way to deal with acting and brought surprising material thriving, the English utilized humor and inconspicuousness?

Obvious experts in the English pop workmanship improvement join Richard Hamilton, Nigel Henderson, and Eduardo Palazzo.

CHAPTER TWO

POP WORKMANSHIP TECHNIQUES AND QUALITIES

We ought to investigate the significant characteristics of pop workmanship that made it such a solid new turn of events. The Sign of Industrialism: Ordered work, use, and authenticity are the essential subjects of pop craftsmanship. Symbols such as grain boxes, Coca-Cola compartments, and Campbell soup compartments are used to convey striking brand names and undeniable product bundling. Pop craftsmanship updated authenticity by showing the overflow of post bellum society through these things.

Limit and Huge name Culture: The obsession with supporting and astounding name culture is another critical subject of pop workmanship. Specialists were likewise consuming Hollywood, motion pictures, magazines, and TV to make works energized by colossal names. Fun reality: Andy Warhol's proverb, "later on, everyone will be unquestionably well known for fifteen minutes," sparked the striking expression "brief involvement in standing." Elvis Presley and Marilyn Monroe were just two of the many pop music virtuosos who were utilized in the plans.

Start to finish correspondence: Makers of pop craftsmanship imitated a large number of sources, including connecting with youth programming, magazines, and TV. They included individuals and things, imitated fascinating shows for youngsters, utilized magazine plans a ton, and once in a while joined pieces of long exchanges into one game plan.

Standard Articles: Standard things found in standard presence found their heading into prestigious pop workmanship designs, an enormous piece of the time with a contemporary, loathing turn. The makers of pop craftsmanship had the choice of raising average things like cheeseburgers, lights, and bananas to the degree of high craftsmanship by utilizing extraordinary social references.

Make and Repeat: One philosophy experts used included standard articles was loosening up the photos to immense degrees and rehashing the photos for lines on end. This made a huge difference and was a mind-blowing certification that brought the topic of bearing home. Imagine an eight-by-four improvement material of colossal Campbell's soup compartments. This was one of Andy Warhol's specific pop craftsmanship styles.

Use Material Wrong: One more method for killing something in mainstream society was to eliminate it from its current circumstance as a different piece or to do it with various things or pictures, contingent upon the subjects of opportunity, reality, and capacity. A massive banana, one of Andy Warhol's famous works, appears on the cover of the presentation collection for The Velvet Underground.

Montage Pictures: Blends are a popular method used in pop art to connect logical elements like photos, text, surfaces, advertising, magazine pages, and plans for comic books. By joining different parts to play on the basic industrialism subjects, pop craftsmanship specialists utilized plans to offer social and imaginative explanations. Hamilton's most fundamental assortment that began the pop craftsmanship improvement joins ceaseless obvious things and people.

Innovative Screen Print Techniques: Screen-print structures, for instance, silkscreen printing and lithography were used by well known experts like Andy Warhol and Roy Lichtenstein to achieve signature pop workmanship looks. Pop art experts also used techniques from broad correspondence symbolism and hitting designs with straight lines and sharp colors.

Overlay, copy, and rehash: Sensible impacts in pop craftsmanship are accomplished through the age, overlay, and duplication of different pictures, whether the work is a social occasion or unquestionable gruffness. Reused symbolism and other overlaid depictions that depicted standard normal presence, things, celebrities, and unmistakable brand names were consistently associated with a few creative groupings.

Sprinkled Tones: Red, blue, yellow, and green with their amazing tones crushed pop craftsmanship plans. Experts expressly used central tones and sprinkled neon tones to convey sureness and flood. The development's success was aided by the vibrant and muted tones of pop art, which went against conventional creative principles. Pop craftsmanship is lovely, blissful, and has a specific measure of internal energy. What ruins you from carrying that whirlwind of imperativeness to your own photos?

1. Exactly when you ship off the application, tap the additional image in the lower right corner of the screen.

2. Move the image to which you should add pop workmanship photo influences.

3. Click on the Effects mechanical social affair at the lower part of your screen.

4. Until you see the Pop Craftsmanship class, investigate extremely absurd. In fact, there is a class on just for pop craftsmanship. You presently have second induction to your re-tried Pop Workmanship generator.

5. Select a Pop Workmanship channel and watch your image change. Take a look at one of our truly Pop Workmanship effects: Pop Workmanship, Off Cross-part, and Glitch2 Tones.

6. Estimating that you should make additional acclimations should the channel, twofold tap on the channel of your choice and change the scales thusly.

7. To save your change, tap Apply in the upper right.

8. Need to add more channels? To pick extra cleaned channels, for instance, the striking Coarseness Impact, return to Impacts, click Pop Workmanship, or select FX. In any case, the layer can have as

many channels as are required. After each change, try to tap Apply.

9. Star tip: Add fun stickers to your image for that pop workmanship plan look. Select a sticker to add to your image by clicking Sticker, entering "Pop craftsmanship" or another pursuit term into the case, and some time later clicking Recovery. You can resize the sticker and make additional updates with the contraptions at the lower part of your screen.

10. Click on the Text contraption, type in the text you really need to add, and some times later pick the heading. You can change the style, arrangement, darkness, and various pieces of the text using the

contraptions at the lower part of your screen.

11. To make various updates, use the Cover, Characteristic of gathering Flare, Shape Cover, and Approaches instruments. For a truly dumbfounding pop craftsmanship influence, we propose attempting Shape Covers.

12. Could it be said that your Pop Craftsmanship picture is satisfactory to you? To save or post, select next in the upper right corner.

If you are looking for a free online photo editor, take a look at the Workspace Changing Contraptions. Explore Sketch Effects, Photo Overlays, Assortment

Receptiveness, and Duotone Effects for some shocking photo changing contraptions guaranteed to make your game arrangement pop.

RULES FOR CHANGING A PICTURE INTO AN ACRYLIC POP WORKMANSHIP PAINTING

There are a lot of destinations that ensure they can change your picture into a work, which basically infers printing it out and using a material. Taking into account everything, why not be helpful times painting it with acrylics? Every single push toward go headings to make a Confined scale Wooden Instrument compartment Christmas Tree Decoration

Survey of the x Tool F1 2-in-1 Double Laser Etcher

Whether you are hoping to light up a generally dull wall or make a customized gift, painting an exceptional thing of beauty is really fulfilling. The accompanying six-step interaction will get your innovative energies pumping and give you imaginative command over the end result.

I'll show you the accompanying:

1. the most effective method to pick the right photo,

2. Instructions to revamp the photograph into a few variety pop craftsmanship picture on your PC utilizing the inventive graphical impacts program Replicators.

3.   The most effective method to add a matrix to the new picture utilizing Microsoft Paint (a free program for Windows computers),

4.   How to draw the image from pop art on a canvas, and finally,   instructions to paint with acrylics. Relax on the off chance that you assume you figure you can't draw or paint since utilizing a matrix to portray the composition typical stunt specialists use to draw precisely and save time makes it simple. This implies that grown-ups and youngsters can appreciate transforming photographs into acrylic pop workmanship compositions.

What you'll need

Mac users can use Paintbrush and Canvas instead of Paint and Replicators.

1. Computerized Supplies

2. Art Supplies

3. A most loved computerized photo

4. A clear extended canvas

5. A plastic paint range

6. A Windows PC computer

7. A ruler

8. A pencil

9. Replicators programming and Microsoft

10. Paint Acrylic

11. Paints

12. Paintbrushes

A note about purchasing the material:
An incredible benefit of this technique is the minimal expense of materials, and that incorporates the material. Materials can be purchased in all shapes and sizes, and assuming you purchase in mass, they will be significantly less expensive (and you have the ideal reason to make more artworks). In the event that you're like me, you like canvases without outlines. Hence, I suggest purchasing a profound edge material otherwise called a "crate material" as opposed to a flimsy casing one since you can involve the stout edges as a

component of the composition for visual allure.

Step 1: Pick a Photo

You presumably have as a primary concern which photo you need to transform into a work of art. I will expect that you have an advanced duplicate of the photograph on your PC; if not, you should make a computerized duplicate of a printed photograph either with a high-goal scanner or by just snapping a picture of the photograph utilizing a high-goal camera.As far as I might be concerned, the photographs that make the best canvases are open activity shots where the subject is regular and uninformed about the camera.

Brightness: The Replicators software will have a hard time identifying lines and shapes if the image is too bright or dark. For instance, a snap taken in full sun without shadows might ease up the skin excessively or add features that make facial highlights hard to characterize.

Contrast: photographs with low difference, like low quality examined pictures, by and large don't function admirably for this activity. Find a different picture if yours looks like it was taken through a dirty window. You will, fortunately, be able to adjust brightness and contrast but if your photo already looks great, you won't need to do much with these settings.

Stage 2: Change the Photograph in Replicators

Replicator is a free and simple to-utilize graphical impacts program for Windows that allows you to make dazzling, proficient designs for both individual and business use. It's great for computerized camera clients and web/visual creators wishing to change photographs into cool pictures without paying a fortune for Photoshop or an expert craftsman. Replicators contains 150 impacts, including Pop Workmanship, Movement Obscure, Sepia, Hallucinogenic Craftsmanship, Andy Warhol, Half-Tone, Spiralize, Ethnic Print, Harsh Sketch, and that's only the tip of the iceberg.

CHAPTER THREE

INSTRUCTIONS TO UTILIZE REPLICATORS TO SET UP THE PHOTOGRAPH

1. Download and introduce Replicators on your PC.

2. Run the Replicators programming. Go to Record and choose Open picture document.

3. Go to the area of your photograph and double tap to open.

4. Each time you open a photograph in Replicators, it will assist you with streamlining the photograph for change. In the first place, change the brilliance and differentiation utilizing the sliders. Change

as fundamental involving the see as an aide and afterward press Straight away.

5. Rotating the image to any angle is the next step. Press Close to move to the following stage.

6. Then, crop the picture. Most of the time, you'll want to crop out parts of a picture that aren't necessary, like in the example below. You will likewise have to guess how your picture will fit onto the material. While editing, remember the elements of the material.

7. After that, select the part of the left image that you want to change with your mouse, and a preview will appear on the

right. Press Close to continue on toward the tomfoolery impacts.

8. To make an exceptional work of art of your photograph utilizing a couple of varieties, utilize the drop-down menu to find and choose Variety Decrease.

9. Press the helpful Next Model button to see what your photograph could resemble after change.

10. Press the Tweak button to move to the following edge and begin to customize your picture with your number one tones.

11. Keep the Shape Width set at nothing and move the Quantity of varieties slider down to a number under 10 however higher than 2.

12. Make sure off (no mixing) is selected from the right-bottom menu.

13. In the event that you are content with the see picture however might want to change tones, just snap on the hued square shapes on the left to pick an alternate tone. This will right away change the review.

14. Press OK to expand the image to the full screen when you are satisfied with the design.

15. Go up to Document and afterward Save picture record. . . put the image somewhere easy to find on your computer, such as on your desktop.

Step 3: Open the Picture in Microsoft Paint

1. On your computer, look for the picture.

2. Right-click on the record and select Open with and afterward select Paint.

On the off chance that you don't have Microsoft Paint, utilize one more basic photograph altering programming on your PC. To open the image in Paintbrush, Mac users can follow the same procedure.

Step 4: Add a Lattice in MS Paint

Back in sync 2, you guessed what lattice size you would have to draw on your fresh start. Make sure to remember both the photograph's and material's aspects when you make your network.

1. Choose a color from the Colors section and select the Line icon from the Shapes toolbar.

2. Place your cursor where you maintain that one level or vertical line should start. Double tap at the ideal area, holding the Shift key down as you drag your cursor across the exercise manual to the contrary side; when you're done, release the Shift key and the mouse. Keep setting level and vertical lines, divided by your inclinations.

3. Go to the document menu and afterward click Save or press Ctrl+S to save your photograph with the total lattice.

Step 5: Using Paint, add a grid to the image.

Sketch Lattice and Each Part's Items Onto Material With a Pencil

1. Measure your grid and lightly draw it onto the canvas with a pencil and a ruler.

2. At the point when the full network is finished, sketch each container from the PC picture onto the material. Try not to stress that the picture you changed in Replicators has a few lopsided edges; simply put forth a valiant effort to see where the layouts of the shapes are and define straight boundaries. With this technique, you can take any crate whenever and sketch it out daintily to

make the total picture. Allow the network to direct you to perceive how the lines in the photograph coordinate. Does a line cross the edge of a crate? Does a line go through the focal point of a crate and afterward straightforwardly up to the top?

TIP: For truly complex areas, you can part one box into four boxes on both the computerized picture and the material. This assists with replicating confounded regions precisely and decrease botches. Pick a box from the digital image and lightly draw it in pencil in the box that corresponds to the canvas. Perceive how I partitioned the most convoluted boxes to catch everything about.

Step 6: Using Replicators, transform the image into a pencil sketch.

Paint a Unique Show-stopper, This is the last and best step of all. After the entirety of your persistent effort of arrangement, you can unwind and appreciate painting your plan. Since your picture just holds back a few tones, you can begin with the lightest variety and paint every one of the areas that ought to be that tone. Put a good amount of paint on your palette, dip your brush in it, and start painting. At the point when you're finished, move to the following tone and fill in those areas. Go on as vital until the haziest variety is finished. You can cover any areas where you went over the lines or filled in an area with the wrong color by painting the darkest areas last. The beauty of pop art is that no matter how precise you are with the brush, your painting will still look great. Acrylic paint is generally sufficiently thick to just require one coat, yet in the event that your pencil lines are as yet noticeable, you should apply a subsequent coat.

TIP: As expressed above, acrylic paints dry quickly, so I recommend that you wash your brushes and paint range following use.

A couple of notes about acrylic paint:

Acrylic paints are perfect for expressions and specialties projects since they dry in a flash, become water-safe when dry, extremely modest to purchase (particularly in bigger sums), keep going quite a while, and by and large needn't bother with to be blended in with different varieties. The special case is dark since it can deliver a sparkling completion when dry contrasted with different tones. Mix it with dark blue or gray before painting it on the canvas to fix this. Although acrylic paint is easy to remove from skin, it will be difficult to remove from clothes if it gets on them. Hence, wearing old garments or a cover while painting is ideal.

One more completed model: A personalized wedding present for my friends—everyone will want one. Admire your masterpiece while you relax. You'll get faster and more creative the more you use this technique. You will start to utilize more intriguing photographs, add more tones, change foundations, etc. The conceivable outcomes are huge. In any case, don't be amazed when your loved ones respect your work such a lot of that they begin requesting that you make compositions for them. You might be able to make extra money from this hobby or just use it to make personalized gifts for birthdays, Christmas, weddings, Mother's Day, Thanksgiving, and other occasions.

CHAPTER FOUR

INSTRUCTIONS TO DRAW POP CRAFTSMANSHIP - A BIT BY BIT GUIDE

Over the course of workmanship, there have been numerous developments and styles that have become cherished by many individuals. Pop Art is a radical new style of art that first appeared in the 1950s. This style would consolidate symbolism from well known comics, items and other such mediums to offer a few unexpected expressions about commercialization. A style and tasteful is well known right up 'til now, and many individuals like to figure out how to attract Pop Craftsmanship to reproduce this style. You will be able to recreate your very own Pop Art piece by the end of this tutorial!

Stage 1

In this guide on the best way to draw Pop Craftsmanship, we will be aiming for a style that frequently incorporates comic book-inspired boards and iconography. Albeit Pop Workmanship can take a wide range of structures, most of them share a typical quality: They are daring, vibrant, and full of color. That will clearly be what is going on for this arrangement, and we will begin by drawing a significant, striking BANG. We will start by attracting each letter huge block letters to truly make it stand apart on the page. This will act as a beginning stage. While drawing these letters, you can put forth a legitimate attempt to reproduce the style we used for our manual for stay with this excellent Pop Workmanship style. In the accompanying several means of the helper, we will focus in on including a couple of extra nuances and around the letters, so when you're set we up will progress forward.

Stage 2

Since you have the letters of the word this plan will focus in on, we can start adding those extra nuances that we referred to for your Pop Workmanship drawing. To do this, we will draw a structure commonly around the letters. This structure will follow the graphs of each letter eagerly, and it will approach one single colossal yet inconsistent shape by and large around the letters. This step can require an all around steady hand if you don't completely accept that this design ought to contact the letters, so make sure to take it continuously as you draw.

Stage 3

For the arrangement we're making in this helper on the most capable technique to draw Pop Craftsmanship, we are hoping to because it to appear to be like the letters are removing the page. In order to achieve this, we will apply a shading effect behind the letters. To do this, you can draw a couple of shapes behind each letter that matches each condition of the letter.

Stage 4

As we referred to around the start of this Pop Workmanship drawing, this style is regularly gigantic and extraordinary, and it will habitually feature severe popping or sensitive imagery. This is a good thing because excellent comic book boards inspire a lot of Pop Craftsmanship. We will add this dangerous impact to this section of the drawing by using a few bent lines that come full circle with sharp tips all around the drawing up to this point. Then, at whatever point this is drawn, you can add another eagerly around the structures of the impact to give it greater significance. Then, at that point, the subsequent stage of the aide's last subtleties and components will be prepared as far as we're concerned.

Stage 5

This fifth step of our helper on the most capable technique to draw Pop Craftsmanship will make them add a last silliness nuances to finish this plan enjoyably. At the point when that is done, you will similarly get the chance to add a couple of fun contemplations of your own. There will be a long, slender, sharp segment at the foundation of every one of these shapes, and there will be a few enormous, adjusted shapes. Go ahead and add your own unique imaginative ideas when these are added. Workmanship is connected to conveying your considerations, so you should genuinely permit your creative mind to stream as you add more nuances or establishment nuances. How should you complete this image before the last step?

Stage 6

Assortment is one of the principal parts of most Pop Craftsmanship, so that is the explanation we will focus in on it for the last step of this Pop Workmanship drawing. We used a couple of brilliant yellows and reds that are balanced for specific more dark blues. While shading, you can experiment with new varieties or even make completely novel selections. Make sure to have a good time as you experiment with various varieties and mediums because changing the workmanship mediums you use will also go a long way toward creating your best image.

4 EXTRA APPROACHES TO MAKING YOUR POP WORKMANSHIP DRAWING NOTEWORTHY

1. Make some workmanship that really pops with these tips for your pop craftsmanship sketch.

2. Pop craftsmanship is known to be colossal and solid, and that is without a doubt shown in this drawing of pop workmanship. By and by, it could constantly be much bolder and bigger.

3. You could do this by adding considerably more parts to the arrangement, for instance, more sharp focuses and impact influences. There is no such thing as going excessively enormous and extraordinary with respect to pop craftsmanship.

4. Pop craftsmanship would as often as possible be awakened by comic book imagery and notification, and you could coordinate some imagery inspired by these sources into your own drawing.

There are various ways you could do this, but one way is draw a comic book character under the image we made in this helper.

Assuming you some way or another ended up doing this; you would be best off using exemplary comics with serious, clean tones accepting you wish to get that pop craftsmanship style. Adding fun workmanship materials and specialties to this pop craftsmanship attracting is one more method for causing it to appear more appealing. For example, you could add stickers, shimmer or even dabs to the image. Remember that the goal with pop workmanship is to make it striking, splendid and empowering! What are a part of your #1 craftsmanship materials that you could use for this masterpiece you have made? This pop craftsmanship sketch we made has the word bang worked out in bile letters. This is again persuaded by parts from model comic books. You could somewhat go with various words to make this image more altered! Blast, POW, or whatever other word that proposes a noisy commotion could be among these. If you need some ideas, you could look up some pages from old comic books. Alternately, you could research examples of pop art craftsmanship that you could use in your own creation. This is such an immortal fine art that many individuals revere, and we trust that this aide on the best way to draw Pop Craftsmanship assisted you with having a great time adding your own twist to the style. We kept up with that this guide ought to make making this show-stopper a horseplay experience as well as one that would be straightforward and that would think about your own inventiveness. Taking into account that, you should accept to change or add to the arrangement in any way you really want! This will be connected to having a few great times getting innovative and we can scarcely keep down to see what you end up with. From that point onward, you can go to our site to gain admittance to an immense library of drawing guides that you can utilize. You should try to check in on a regular basis because we frequently change them.

THE END